T4-ABN-842

Team Stats—Football Edition

HIGHLIGHTS OF THE PITTSBURGH STEELERS

MARYSA STORM

BLACK RABBIT BOOKS

Bolt is published by Black Rabbit Books
P.O. Box 3263, Mankato, Minnesota, 56002.
www.blackrabbitbooks.com
Copyright © 2019 Black Rabbit Books

Jennifer Besel, editor; Grant Gould & Michael Sellner, designers; Omay Ayres, photo researcher

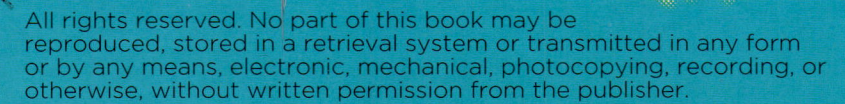

All rights reserved. No part of this book may be reproduced, stored in a retrieval system or transmitted in any form or by any means, electronic, mechanical, photocopying, recording, or otherwise, without written permission from the publisher.

Library of Congress Cataloging-in-Publication Data
Names: Storm, Marysa, author.
Title: Highlights of the Pittsburgh Steelers / by Marysa Storm.
Description: Mankato, Minnesota : Black Rabbit Books, 2019. | Series: Bolt. Team stats. Football edition | Includes bibliographical references and index.
Identifiers: LCCN 2017049431 (print) | LCCN 2017052306 (ebook) | ISBN 9781680725537 (e-book) | ISBN 9781680724370 (library binding) | ISBN 9781680727319 (paperback)
Subjects: LCSH: Pittsburgh Steelers (Football team)—History—Juvenile literature.
Classification: LCC GV956.P57 (e-book) | LCC GV956.P57 S86 2019 (print) | DDC 796.332/640974886—dc23
LC record available at https://lccn.loc.gov/2017049431

Printed in China. 3/18

Image Credits

Alamy: Doug Schneider, 3, 16–17, 22–23 (bkgd); ZUMA Press, Inc., 16–17 (Parker); AP Images: AP, 7; David Durochik, 19 (b); Hall of Fame via AP, 6; NFL/LIEBB, 10, 19 (t); Vernon Biever, 18; commons.wikimedia.org: 12–13 (trophy); Getty: Focus on Sport, 14 (t), 21 (both), 25; Heinz Kluetmeier, 9; Kevin C. Cox, 4–5; Rick Stewart, 17 (Roethisberger); The Sporting News, 24; Walter Iooss Jr., 12–13 (game), 20; Shutterstock: enterlinedesign, 28–29 (ball); Orgus88, 14 (ball); Svyatoslav Aleksandrov, 31; VitaminCo, 10, 32 (ball); USA TODAY Sports: Denny Medley, 1; Williams, 28–29 (t); James Lang, Cover; Jim Matthews, 26

Every effort has been made to contact copyright holders for material reproduced in this book. Any omissions will be rectified in subsequent printings if notice is given to the publisher.

CONTENTS

CHAPTER 1
On the Field.........4

CHAPTER 2
History of
the Steelers...........7

CHAPTER 3
Greatest Moments....11

CHAPTER 4
Stars of the Steelers..18

Other Resources..........30

CHAPTER 1

On the FIELD

It was the 2009 Super Bowl. The Pittsburgh Steelers' **opponents** led by just three points. But less than a minute of the game remained. Steelers' quarterback Ben Roethlisberger launched a pass. Wide receiver Santonio Holmes leapt into the air. He caught the ball. Touchdown! The team won its sixth Super Bowl!

Touchdown!

5

The team was originally called the Pittsburgh Pirates.

6

CHAPTER 2

HISTORY
of the Steelers

The Steelers is one of the NFL's most successful teams. But it took the team time to reach the top. Art Rooney started the team in 1933. Its first seven years were rough. The team went through five head coaches. It only won 22 games.

A Record-Making Team

The team didn't win its first **division** title until 1972. That's when things took off for the team. With Chuck Noll as coach, the team won the 1975 Super Bowl. It went on to win the big game in 1976, 1979, and 1980. The Steelers won again in 2006 and 2009. No team has more Super Bowl victories.

Most Super Bowl Appearances
as of 2017 season

New England Patriots	10
Dallas Cowboys	8
Denver Broncos	8
Pittsburgh Steelers	8
San Francisco 49ers	6

Chuck Noll

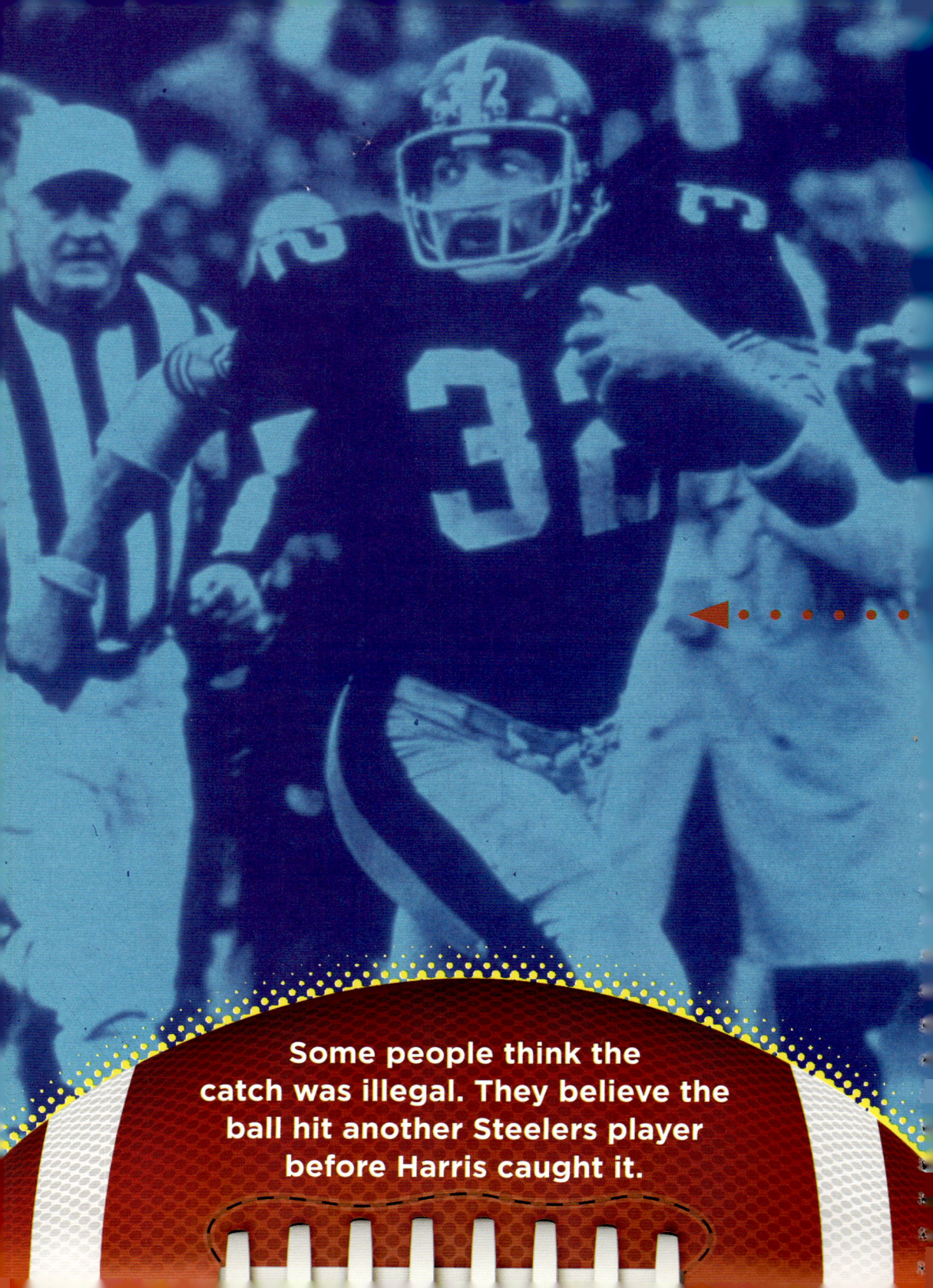

Some people think the catch was illegal. They believe the ball hit another Steelers player before Harris caught it.

CHAPTER 3

Greatest MOMENTS

Steelers' history is full of big moments. In 1972, the Steelers faced the Oakland Raiders in a **playoff** game. The Raiders led by one point with less than a minute left. The Steelers had the ball. Quarterback Terry Bradshaw threw a pass. His teammate leaped up to catch it, but a Raider blocked it. The ball bounced off one of them. Franco Harris rushed to the ball. He caught it before it hit the ground. Then he rushed in for a touchdown. The Steelers won 13–7!

1975 Super Bowl

The Steelers won its first Super Bowl in 1975. It beat the Minnesota Vikings 16–6. The Steelers' **defense** pounded the Vikings. The Vikings only gained 119 yards the entire game.

13

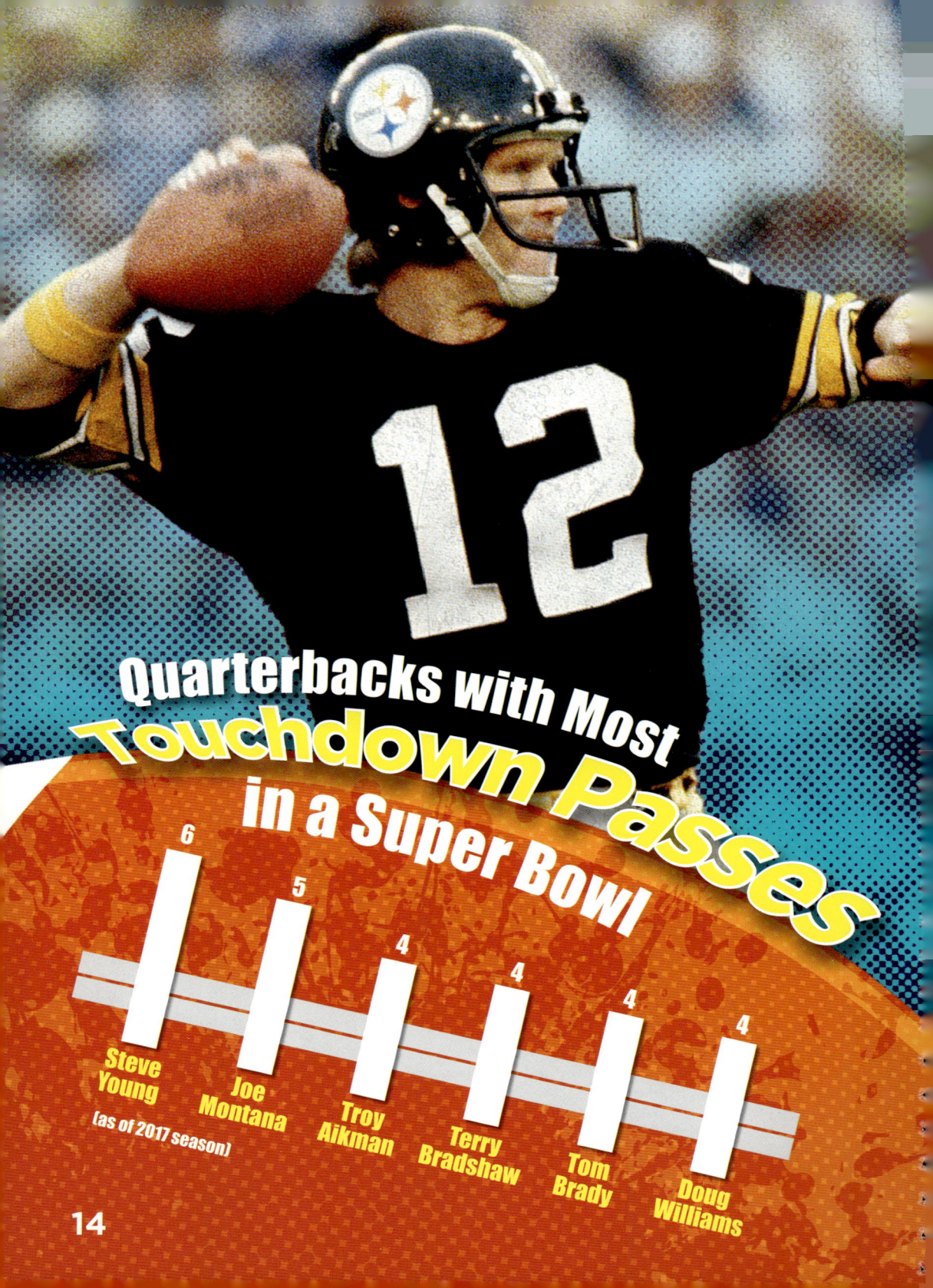

Quarterbacks with Most Touchdown Passes in a Super Bowl

- Steve Young — 6 (as of 2017 season)
- Joe Montana — 5
- Troy Aikman — 4
- Terry Bradshaw — 4
- Tom Brady — 4
- Doug Williams — 4

14

1979 Super Bowl

The team went to its third Super Bowl in 1979. It played the Cowboys. During the game, Bradshaw threw four touchdown passes. Few quarterbacks have made that many in one Super Bowl. Bradshaw became the game's **MVP**.

BY THE NUMBERS

total retired jersey numbers: 2

75 yards longest Super Bowl rush (Steelers player Willie Parker)

23 years old

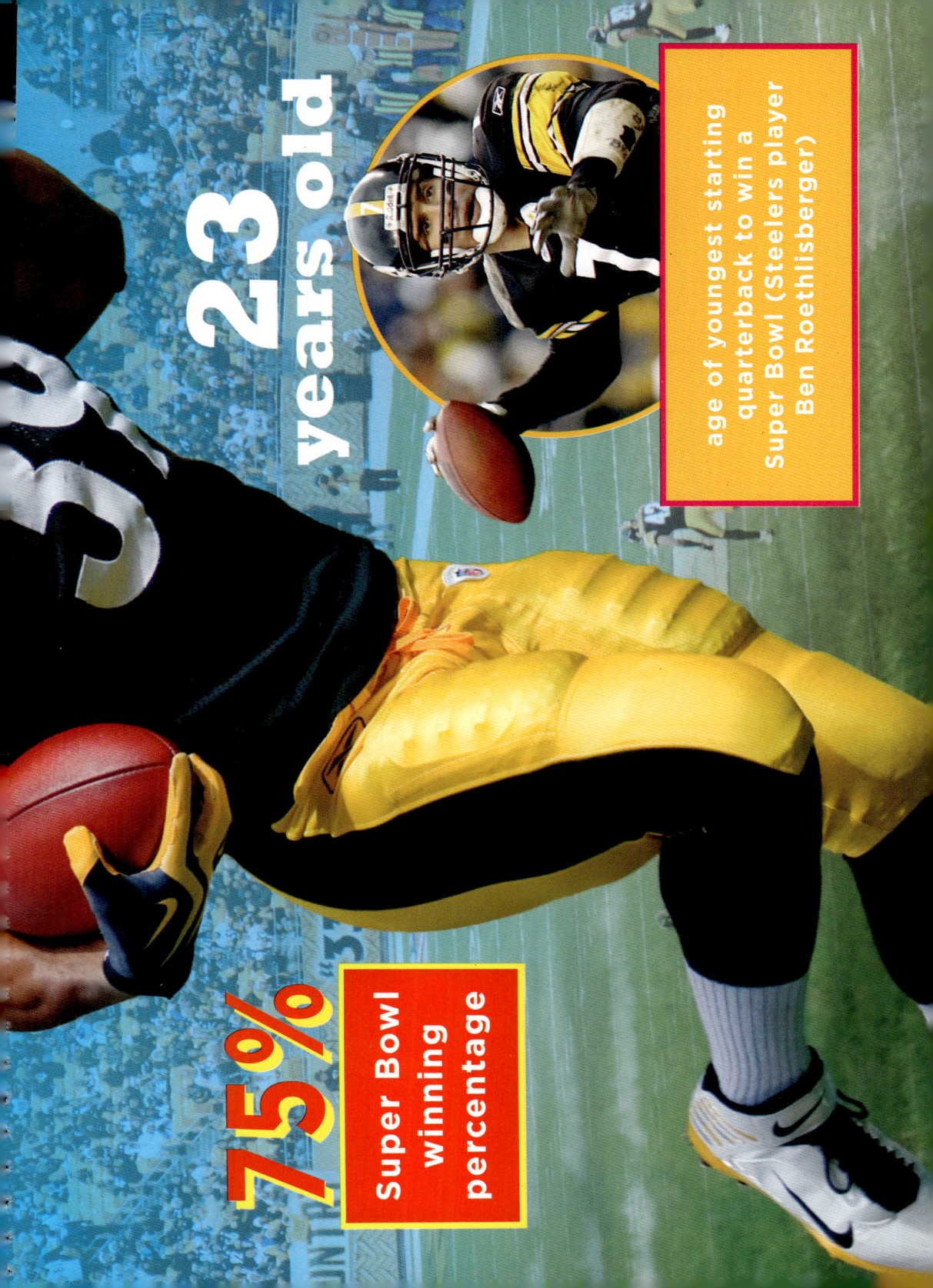

age of youngest starting quarterback to win a Super Bowl (Steelers player Ben Roethlisberger)

75% Super Bowl winning percentage

CHAPTER 4

STARS
of the Steelers

The Steelers has seen many amazing players. Franco Harris was a star running back. He made 100 touchdowns for the Steelers. He won some big awards during his **career**.

Harris' Awards

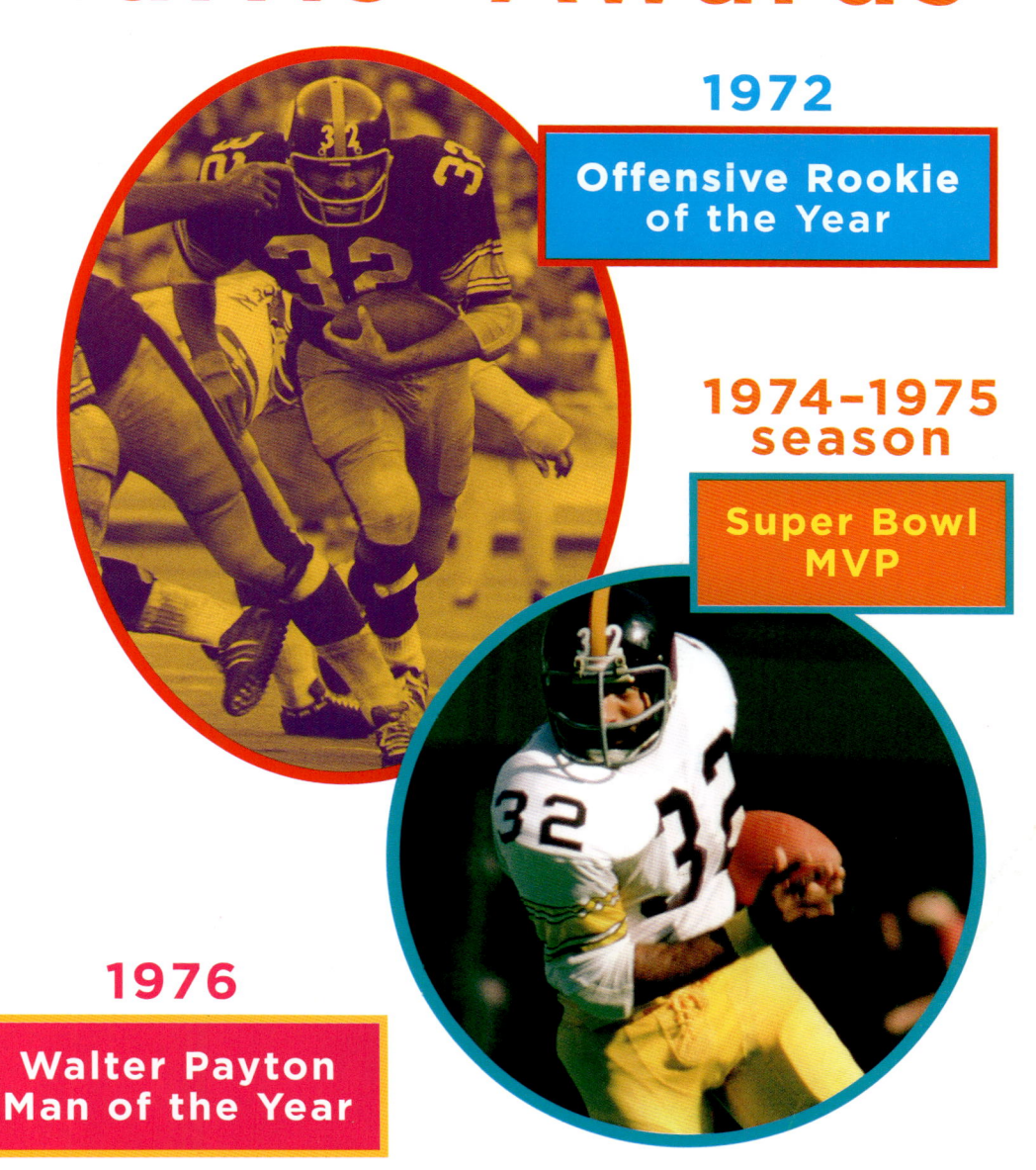

1972
Offensive Rookie of the Year

1974–1975 season
Super Bowl MVP

1976
Walter Payton Man of the Year

Terry Bradshaw

A beast on the field, Bradshaw led the Steelers to many victories. His strong passes helped the team win four Super Bowls. He was MVP of two of them. Bradshaw retired with 212 passing touchdowns.

Quarterbacks with the Most Super Bowl Wins (through 2017 season)

TOM BRADY	5
TERRY BRADSHAW	4
JOE MONTANA	4
TROY AIKMAN	3

Joe Greene

"Mean" Joe Greene played defensive tackle. He was the 1969 Defensive Rookie of the Year. Greene was quick and strong. He was a strong leader on the famous Steel Curtain Defense.

THE STEEL CURTAIN
The Steelers' 1970s defense was like a wall. Other teams couldn't break it down. Fans called the defense the Steel Curtain.

- Mel Blount
- Glen Edwards
- Joe Greene
- L.C. Greenwood
- Jack Ham
- Ernie Holmes
- Jack Lambert
- Andy Russell
- Mike Wagner
- Dwight White

pounds   30   60   90

SUPER BOWLS THE STEEL CURTAIN HELPED WIN:
1975, 1976, 1979, AND 1980

POINTS ALLOWED BY THE ▸
STEEL CURTAIN DEFENSE

Sizing Them Up: Stars of the Steel Curtain

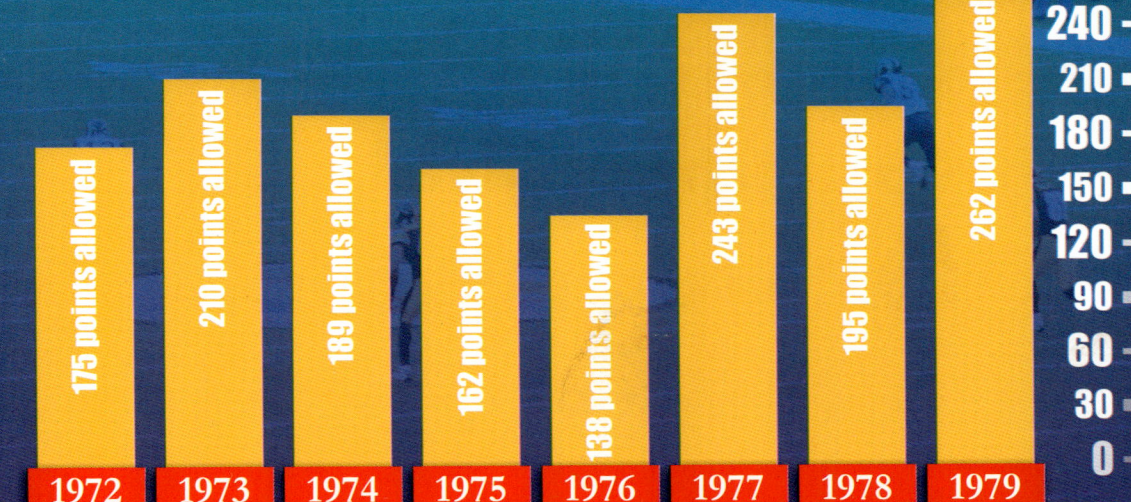

- 205 pounds (93 kilograms)
- 185 pounds (84 kg)
- 275 pounds (125 kg)
- 245 pounds (111 kg)
- 225 pounds (102 kg)
- 260 pounds (118 kg)
- 220 pounds (100 kg)
- 225 pounds (102 kg)
- 210 pounds (95 kg)
- 255 pounds (116 kg)

120　150　180　210　240　270

1972 season	175 points allowed
1973 season	210 points allowed
1974 season	189 points allowed
1975 season	162 points allowed
1976 season	138 points allowed
1977 season	243 points allowed
1978 season	195 points allowed
1979 season	262 points allowed

Jack Lambert

Jack Lambert was a linebacker. He was tough. In fact, fans call him one of the toughest linebackers. He made 17 fumble recoveries.

Jack Lambert	VS.	Jack Ham
46	games played	62
28	interceptions	32
17	fumble recoveries	21

Jack Ham

Jack Ham also played linebacker. He had speed and intelligence. He always seemed to be in the right place at the right time.

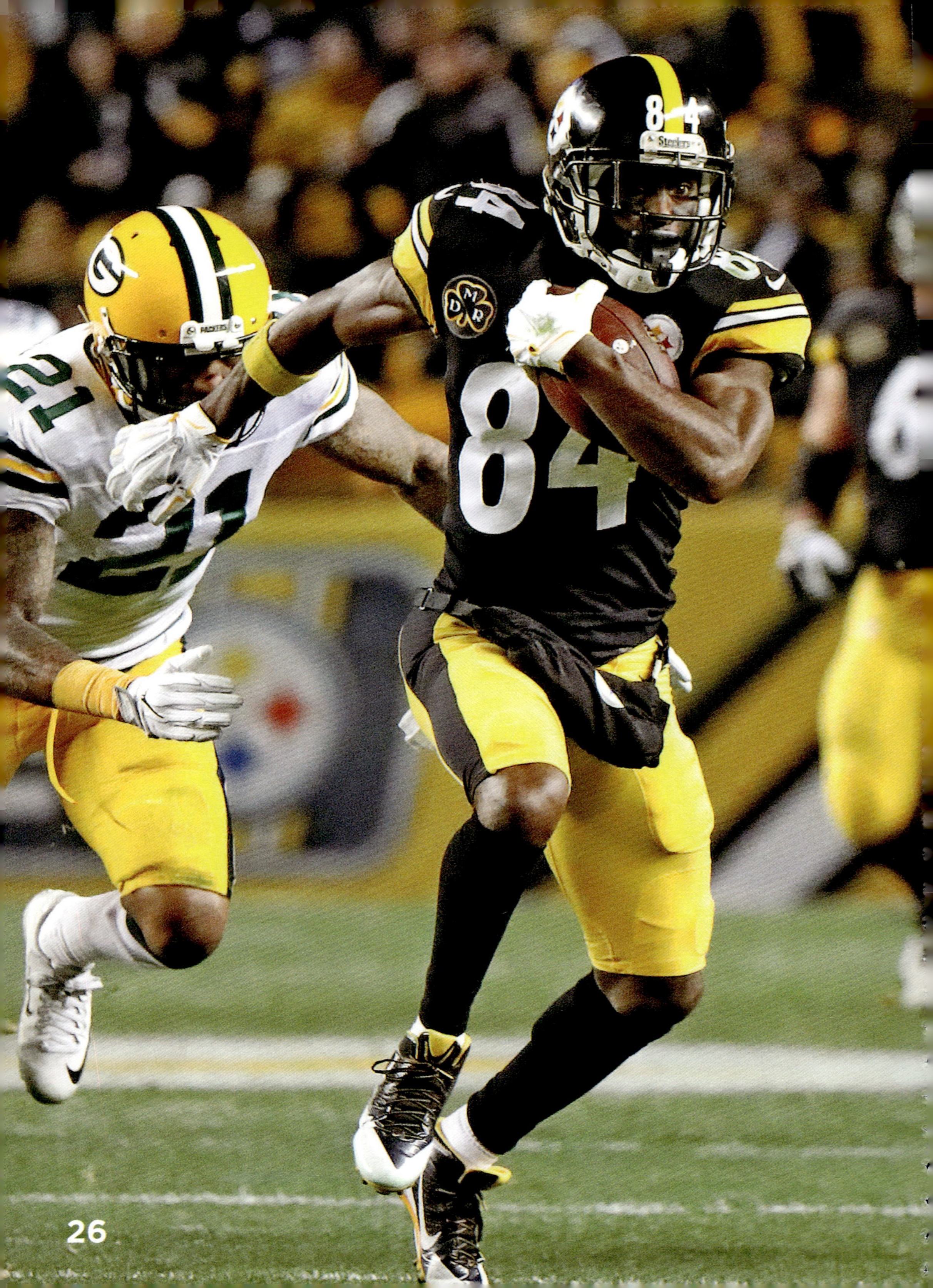

Antonio Brown

Antonio Brown plays wide receiver. With unbelievable energy, he races past defenders. He was the Steelers' MVP in 2011, 2013, and 2015. Brown ranked fourth in the NFL's top 100 players of 2017.

Fans can't wait to see what the team does next. Who knows? Maybe it'll win a seventh Super Bowl.

TIMELINE

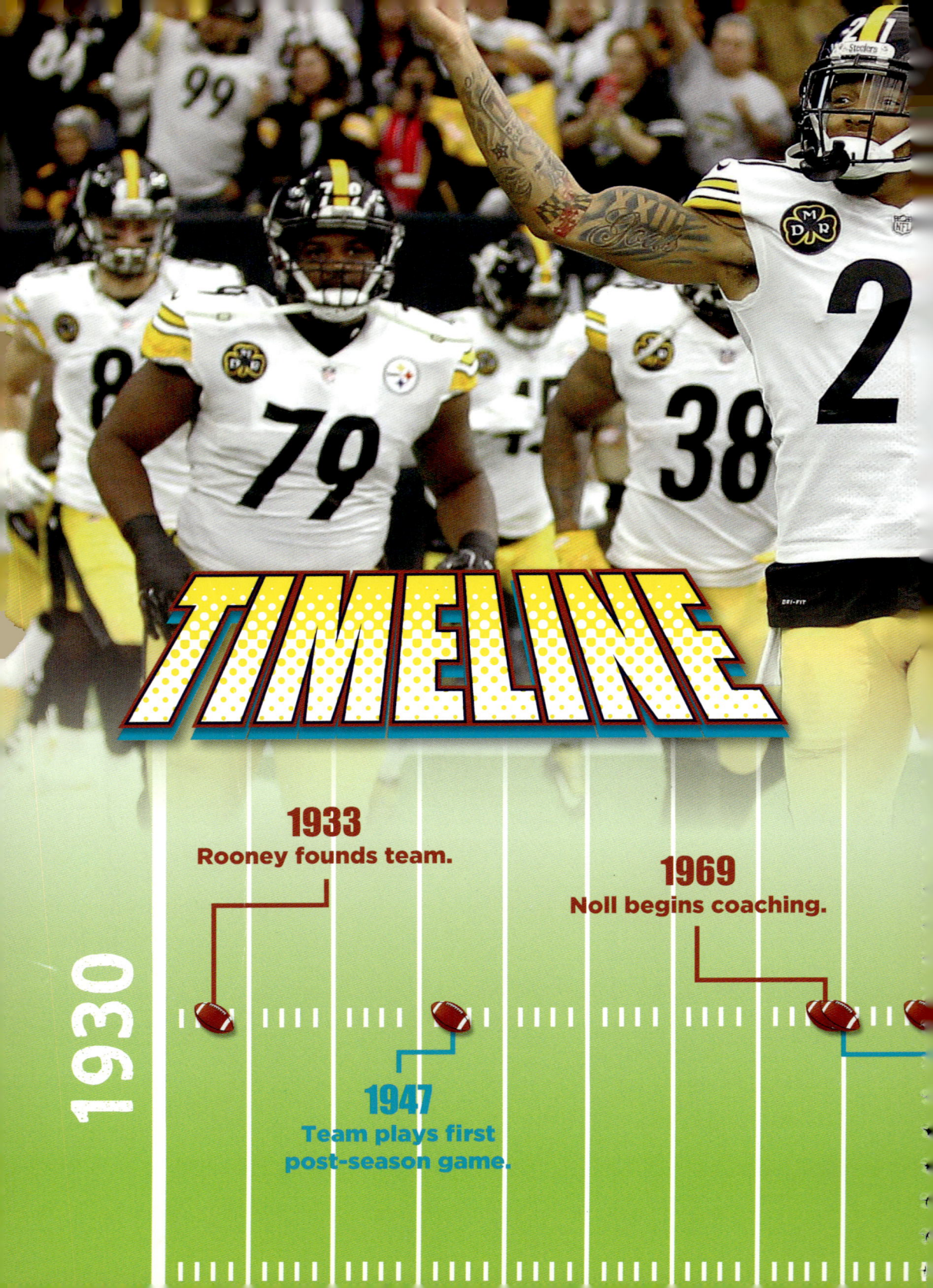

1930

1933
Rooney founds team.

1947
Team plays first post-season game.

1969
Noll begins coaching.

1975
Team wins first Super Bowl.

2017
NFL ranks Brown one of the top 100 players of the year.

1970s
Steel Curtain defense dominates.

2009
Team wins sixth Super Bowl.

2020

GLOSSARY

career (kuh-REER)—a period of time spent in a job

defense (DEE-fens)—the players on a team who try to stop the other team from scoring

division (duh-VIH-zuhn)—a competitive class or category

MVP—an award given to the best player in the league each season; MVP stands for most valuable player.

offensive (OH-fen-sive)—relating to the attempt to score in a game

opponent (uh-POH-nunt)—a person, team, or group that is competing against another

playoff (PLAY-ahf)—a series of games played after the regular season to decide which player or team is the champion

retire (ree-TIYR)—to stop playing a game or competition; it also means to withdraw from use.

rookie (ROOK-ee)—a first-year player

LEARN MORE

BOOKS

Burgess, Zack. *Meet the Pittsburgh Steelers.* Big Picture Sports. Chicago: Norwood House Press, 2017.

Graves, Will. *Pittsburgh Steelers.* NFL Up Close. Minneapolis: SportsZone, an imprint of Abdo Publishing, 2017.

Osborne, M.K. *Superstars of the Pittsburgh Steelers.* Pro Sports Superstars NFL. Mankato, MN: Amicus, 2019.

WEBSITES

Football: National Football League
www.ducksters.com/sports/national_football_league.php

NFL RUSH
www.nflrush.com

Official Site of the Pittsburgh Steelers
www.steelers.com

INDEX

B
Bradshaw, Terry, 11, 14, 15, 20
Brown, Antonio, 27, 29

G
Greene, Joe, 21, 22–23

H
Ham, Jack, 22–23, 24, 25
Harris, Franco, 10, 11, 18–19
history, 4, 6, 7, 8, 10, 11, 12, 15, 28–29

L
Lambert, Jack, 22–23, 24

N
Noll, Chuck, 8, 28

R
Roethlisberger, Ben, 4, 17

S
Steel Curtain defense, 21, 22–23, 28–29
Super Bowls, 4, 8, 12, 14, 15, 16, 17, 19, 20, 27, 29